STREET BIKES

30 YEARS OF HIGH PERFORMANCE MOTORCYCLES

STREET BIKES

30 YEARS OF HIGH PERFORMANCE MOTORCYCLES

MARK ZIMMERMAN

PHOTOGRAPHY BY JEFF HACKETT

Crescent Books

New York/Avenel, New Jersey

Acknowledgments

Special thanks go to Karen Berman, who edited the text; Beth Crowell, who designed the book and the book jacket; and Judith Kip, who prepared the index.

To acknowledge each and every individual who helped make this book a reality would require at least another chapter. Unfortunately that is not possible.

All of the motorcycles profiled were provided by their owners, who kindly rearranged their schedules and made their bikes available on short notice in order to accommodate us.

One of motorcycling's greatest pleasures is its camaraderie, without which this book would not have been possible. To all of those who provided bikes, information and most importantly, moral support, a profound and heartfelt thanks.

Jeff and Mark

Page 1 The Norton 750 Commando.
Page 2 A 1986 Suzuki GSX-R1100.
Below A 1976 Moto Guzzi 850 LeMans.

This 1995 edition published by Crescent Books, distributed by Random House Value Publishing, Inc., 40 Engelhard Avenue
Avenel, New Jersey 07001

Random House
New York • Toronto • London • Sydney • Auckland

Produced by
Brompton Books Corporation,
15 Sherwood Place
Greenwich, CT 06830

ISBN 0-517-12185-9

8 7 6 5 4 3 2 1

Printed and bound in Spain

TABLE OF CONTENTS

Introduction

In an industry as often noted for its conservatism as its innovation (at least in its early years), there have always been forward-thinking motorcycle designers willing to risk it all on one roll of the two-wheeled dice. And so it was for the men who created the high performance street bike – the superbike.

The term superbike is a relatively new one. Coined by the motorcycle press in the early 1970s, it was first used to describe the new generation of big-bore road-going motorcycles that appeared on the roads in the late 1960s and early 1970s. Bikes such as the Norton Commando, the Triumph Trident, the BMW /5 series and the Honda CB750 were so much better than their predecessors that they indeed seemed to be "super" bikes.

While the term superbike itself might be relatively new, the definition isn't. The names Turner, Brough, Irving and Vincent should ring a bell, as should Crocker, Davidson, Honda, Friz and Taglioni – all of which were among the earliest to break the mold.

Arguably, the first high performance bike was the Brough Superior. Handsome, wickedly fast, rare and expensive, Broughs were built from 1919 to 1940. In the United States, the Crocker was probably the most awe-inspiring bike of the 1930s. Hand-built in small numbers, Al Crocker's V-twin debuted in 1936. The Crocker, like the Brough, was fast, well-made and high priced. For various reasons, mostly economical, neither was an outstanding commercial success.

The problem with the Brough and the Crocker had been that though they were magnificent performers, they were financially out of reach for all but the wealthiest riders. Besides, their rarity made them impractical for any kind of normal usage – it wasn't as if there was a Brough agent on every corner, or even in every country.

The first superbike to command widespread public acceptance was the Edward Turner-designed 1937 Triumph Speed Twin. The Speed Twin changed the world's (or at least Europe's) perception of what a motorcycle should be. Here was a motorcycle that was not only handsome, fast and reliable, but at around £75, was also comfortably affordable. The Speed Twin revolutionized motorcycling; it set a new standard. You could ride this bike to work on Monday through Friday, take your sweetheart to the show on it on Saturday and race it on Sunday.

True, other manufacturers had bikes that could be pressed into the same kind of service; most of the British marques offered machines as capable, at least in theory, as the Speed Twin. Some were V-twins, some were singles, and one – the Rudge Ulster – even had a four-valve head; however, none have proven as enduring a design as the Speed Twin, and for that, the Speed Twin gets my vote as the first real superbike.

With the advent of the new Triumph, European designers immediately picked up on the new trend. In 1938, BSA released its first Gold Star, Norton had its International, Velocette had its overhead cam KTS and Vincent was well on its way to becoming a legend with its first V-twin, the series "A" (actually released late in 1937). In the United States, Harley-Davidson and Indian went at it fiercely; the market for new bikes was minuscule and every dollar meant another day of survival. Both companies built large, side-valve motorcycles, which while comfortable and reliable, were not as technically advanced as their British and continental rivals.

The Second World War put a stop to most if not all motorcycle development for quite a while. Technological advances made during the war, as well as a vastly changed social and political structure, would have an effect on motorcycling that has lasted to this day.

ABOVE Edward Turner's masterpiece, the 1938 Triumph Speed Twin. Had Turner done nothing else, his place in motorcycling history would have been secure. Never before had styling and performance been so perfectly matched.

LEFT The Harley-Davidson "Knuckle Head" had a large, slow-revving engine, big soft tires and floor boards. The antithesis of a "sporting motorcycle," it was, however, well suited to America's wide open spaces and long straight roads.

After the war, the rapid advances in metallurgy, mechanical design and manufacturing techniques that had proven so vital to all sides in the war were translated directly into the next generation of motorcycles. Designers quickly adapted to the new order; hydraulic forks replaced girders, rear shock absorbers replaced rigid frames (an idea that apparently escaped Turner for a short time), and aluminum alloy began to replace cast iron.

In Europe, especially England, the Vincent was king of the hill and would remain so until 1955, when the factory closed: The Vincent, like the Brough and the Crocker before it, simply cost too much to make. Meanwhile, when Indian closed up shop in 1953, Harley-Davidson found itself in the enviable position of being the sole American manufacturer of motorcycles, a situation that more or less exists to this day.

The war had changed more than the game, however – it had also changed the players. Japan, which had been devastated by the war, needed cheap mass transportation, and what was better than a motorbike to negotiate the war-ravaged countryside? Japanese

manufacturers had been building motorcycles since the early 1930s, but it wasn't until after the war that they seriously considered manufacturing them on a large scale. By the late 1950s, Soichiro Honda and the other Japanese motorcycle manufacturers had become highly competitive.

Italy's motorcycle industry had always enjoyed strong protective home-market tariffs. This allowed its designers to concentrate most of their energies on Grand Prix bikes and on small-bore street-going replicas of the GPs. In Italy, the upstart Ducati would soon make the word desmodromic known, if not exactly understood.

As the 1950s came to a close, the Japanese and Italians were battling for small-bore supremacy, much as they are now for the superbike crown. The British, by nature somewhat conservative, continued to develop their postwar singles and twins incrementally. The Germans, with their typical attention to detail, produced well-crafted if somewhat sober machines, though some showed surprising performance. The Americans kept plodding along with their basic V-twins, improving them year by year, more

intent on building a reliable, comfortable machine than one with sporting pretensions.

By 1959, the first of the modern superbikes had emerged: the Triumph Bonneville, a direct descendant of the original Speed Twin. The Bonny was realistically capable of an honest 120 mph, it handled nicely and it stopped reasonably well. It was reliable and easy to maintain. Over the next decade, the T120, as it was officially known, would only get better, reaching its pinnacle in the 1970 model.

Performance twins from Norton and BSA were hot on the Triumph's heels, as was the Harley-Davidson Sportster, which had been designed to meet the emerging American desire for a lighter, "hotter" British-style motorcycle. The BMW R69S, while rather staid compared to the British bikes and the H-D, offered a surprising amount of performance for so civilized a motorcycle. From Italy came a host of small performance bikes, pocket superbikes, if you will, 250cc models that could reach 100 mph and race-bred 175cc and 125cc models. From the Far East,

the Honda Hawk and Super Hawk were notable. The small Japanese two-strokes, while basically improved versions of the German Adler, DKW, and MZ designs, were equally sophisticated. Names like Honda, Yamaha, Suzuki and Kawasaki were soon on the tongues of motorcyclists the world over.

All of the bikes in this book were chosen because they are super street bikes. Some were chosen for what they were, some for what they became and some because emotion (either mine or the designers') triumphed over good sense. All of these motorcycles were commercially available between January 1, 1965, and January 1, 1995. While some were made in limited numbers, there are none that weren't for sale to the general public. I feel that each of these high performance street bikes has made an outstanding contribution to the sport of motorcycling.

— *Mark Zimmerman*

The Triumph Bonneville

The lineal descendant of the original 500cc Speed Twin, the 650cc Bonneville was a true superbike in every sense of the word. The 650 was introduced in direct response to the American market's incessant clamor for more power. Fearful that traditional methods of increasing horsepower – radical cams, larger valves, bigger carbs and the like – would compromise the T100's reputation for reliability, Turner, heeding the old tuner's adage that there's no substitute for cubic inches, simply decided to design a new, larger engine.

The first 650 was the 6T, or Thunderbird. While on the surface it might have appeared to be simply a larger version of the 500, it was its own motorcycle. On September 20, 1949, the first three 6Ts to come off the assembly line were ridden directly from the factory to the English Channel ferry, ferried across to France, and ridden to the Montlhery racetrack, near Paris. The bikes were then ridden side by side for 500 miles at an average speed of over 90 mph, including a final lap at over 100! Then they were ridden back to the factory to be cleaned up and displayed at the Earl's Court show in London. It was a master stroke of public relations – no one had ever attempted a stunt like it before, and no one else would for a long time to come.

The Thunderbird was released as a 1950 model and was a huge seller, particularly in the United States. It could cruise at 90 mph for hours on end, but was a tractable and personable machine around town. American tuners loved it; it was strong and responded well to the same kind of massaging that had worked to such good advantage on its smaller brothers.

Four years later, the Tiger 110 was born (110 stood for 110 mph). It was an even bigger success. In tests, the T110 often achieved speeds approaching 120 mph. The Tiger had a higher compression ratio than the T-Bird, as well as larger valves and ports and the cam profile needed to make it all work – the highly desirable, Q-grind-E3325-sports camshaft, as it was listed in the parts book. Still equipped with a single carb, the T110 had as much performance as most riders would ever need.

One rider who apparently needed a little more was Johnny Allen of Fort Worth, Texas. He rode his modified and streamlined Thunderbird-based bike to an incredible 214 mph at the Bonneville Salt Flats in 1956. The bike, built by Texas Triumph dealer Pete Dalio, tuner Jack Wilson and designer Stormy Mangham, was the first Triumph to hold the overall world speed record, but it wouldn't be the last. Demand for more performance continued unabated, and in view of Allen's feat, was it any wonder? More and more performance "goodies" became available from the factory, including the famous "race kits." In

RIGHT The '65 Bonneville. The single leading shoe front brake was a bit weak, considering the speeds that the Bonny was capable of. The '65 model is slightly detuned compared to the later models.

OPPOSITE The placement of the luggage rack on the top of the tank on the '65 Bonny was questionable, but everything else was spot on. The '65 specifications included dual Amal 1-1/8 monobloc carburetors and 8.5-to-1 compression, just the ticket for the "World's Fastest Motorcycle."

1955, the first twin carb head appeared. These "delta" heads, as they were known, proved to be the hot tip; the Bonny was waiting in the wings.

"The Decision," as factory service manager J.R. Nelson termed it, was made in late 1958, so late that the sales brochure for 1959 didn't even list Triumph's new flagship; only a late price list mentioned the new dual-carb model, the T120 Bonneville.

In 1965, the Bonny was at the top of its class. In time, it would get an improved front fork and brake and concentric carbs would replace the monoblocks. The T120R, while undergoing continual improvement, remained true to its original concept – a motorcycle as much at home touring two-up across the highway as it was on the racetrack, a bike capable of winning road races, scrambles and flattrack, or just as happily running out to do a few errands.

A few short years later, in 1970, the Bonneville peaked. New designs surpassed it. Although the Bonny would eventually displace 750cc and acquire a five-speed transmission and dual-disc brakes, it would never again attain the status it held in the 1960s when it was, to quote the factory, "The Best Motorcycle in the World."

LEFT AND BELOW First released in 1973, the 750cc T140's were the final incarnation of the Bonneville line. All T140's used an oil bearing frame and five-speed transmission. Early models had a front disc and rear drum brake, as well as a right side shift lever. In 1976 new U.S. regulations mandated a left side shifter; a rear disc brake was added at the same time. Parallel intake port heads, Amal MK11 carburetors and electronic ignition (hence the "E") were added in 1979 to meet U.S. emission requirements. This 1979 T140E has an aftermarket exhaust (U.S.-made "BUB's") and Marzocchi rear shocks.

The Harley-Davidson Sportster

BELOW The motorcycle that separates the men from the boys: the H-D 900cc Sportster. The example shown here is an "H" model. Note the large tank and the detuned engine on this civilized version of one of the best street fighters of all time.

OPPOSITE Unique to the Sportster "H", an electric starter is hidden behind the rear cylinder. These machines had lots of chrome and plenty of go.

By the end of the 1940s, Harley-Davidson, and to a lesser extent, Indian Motorcycles, realized that they were losing ground rapidly to British and continental manufacturers. During the war, many young, motorcycle-oriented GIs had discovered that British and continental motorcycles were lighter, faster, better handling and easier to ride than the American bikes then on the market. The returning GIs wanted those bikes, and more and more were imported every year to satisfy them. Harley-Davidson attacked the British (who were really the only ones doing any motorcycle business in America at the time) on two fronts. On May 15, 1951, the H-D Motor Company went to the U.S. Congress and asked for both a sales quota to keep the British machines out, and a 40 percent tax on the ones that came in. They were denied.

Meanwhile, their dealers demanded a new "mid-dle-weight" machine capable of meeting the British "threat" head on. The first "K" model was released in 1952: a 750 flathead, with front and rear suspension and a foot shift, all new innovations for H-D at the time. While the bike was pretty and handled well enough, it was dead slow; any good 500 overhead valve engine of the day could run away from it in a heartbeat. In 1954 they released the 900cc version, the KH. On a good day it might have kept up with a 500, but that's about all. By 1956 the K's were dropped from the line-up.

Then, in 1957, one of the most sought-after motorcycles of all time was born – the 900cc overhead valve Sportster-XL.

Initially, the Sportster was sold as a sport/roadster kind of bike. Factory options were saddlebags, windshields, luggage racks and, in typical Harley fashion, about six tons of chrome. None of it could hide the Sportster's awesome power. In 1958, the factory offered a stripped-down version; the lights, battery and mufflers were left off and in their place went a magneto, high straight pipes and a small 2.25-gallon "peanut" tank. This bike was called the XLC, and for an additional $60, the dealer would install mufflers, lights and a small battery, making the XLC street legal. The factory strategists, realizing a good thing when they saw it, began manufacturing the XLCH (contrary to legend, the "CH" doesn't stand for "competition-hot" or "California-highway," but what it does stand for the factory has never said). Lean, mean and rattlesnake tough, the CH quickly earned a reputation as an ornery street fighter. While the overall performance was about the same as a good Bonneville, Lightning (BSA) or Atlas (yet certainly less than that of an average Vincent), its 900cc worth of torque endowed it with straight-line accelerative capabilities that had to be experienced to be believed. The CH, with its small tank and firm seat, was the perfect

ABOVE A completely stock "H", saddlebags and all, was still faster than many pure sport bikes. The rear shocks are canted forward to clear the saddlebags, making for a firm ride. The shorty mufflers are surprisingly quiet.

"TT" (tavern to tavern) racer. Wheel stands, smoky burnouts and lots of *Sturm und Drang* were its real forte. If you wanted something more civilized, there was always the plain "H" model or an Electra Glide.

By 1972, the Sportster would displace a full liter; however, by then it would be an anachronism, slow, heavy and as vibratory as a jackhammer. It would also lose its mag and eventually gain an electric start. By 1979, the CH as a separate entity would be gone.

The CH sired a remarkable number of offspring, not all of them made by H-D. The prettiest, the

short-lived cafe-racer-style XLCR was made only during 1976 and 1977. It was not a good seller, although it's considered collectible now. In 1983, the factory released the XR1000, the fastest over-the-counter Sportster ever made. It consisted of the top end of the XR750 (the factory race engine) mated to the standard XL's bottom end and equipped with dual carbs and high pipes. The XR1000 was a good example of what H-D could do. Unfortunately, the timing wasn't right for its release, and it was not a popular seller. Today it is a highly collectible bike.

LEFT The "H" wears a small headlamp shroud and the optional windshield. The crash bars and right side mirror were also options.

BELOW The chrome piece between the "jugs" (cylinders) is the horn.

BOTTOM The pilot's eye view of the "H". The wiring for the kill and horn buttons as well as the throttle cable are neatly routed through the handlebars. The tachometer was an option; only the speedometer was standard.

The Norton Commando

RIGHT The 1972 Norton
Commando Roadster. Lots
of shiny alloy, non-unit
construction and the typical
British "bits and pieces"
approach to construction
typify the Commando. The
round piece just forward
of the foot peg bracket is the
pivot point for the swingarm.
The shims for the Isolastic
mount are located between
the swingarm and the
subframe.

OPPOSITE The Commando's
mufflers are the distinctive
"pea shooters." The large
knobs on the top of the
shocks hold the seat on.

PAGE 22 The forerunner
of the Commando was the
highly desirable Dunstall
version of the Atlas. Paul
Dunstall modified the already
hot Atlas motor with his
own cams, big bore kits and
other speed bits. He installed
disc brakes and custom
bodywork to create a fast,
well-handling bike for the
street and track.

The introduction of the Norton Commando at the 1967 Earl's Court show should have dispelled for all time the old adage against teaching old dogs new tricks. Here was the hoary old Atlas power plant, cloaked in a new frame and body work unlike anything that had ever rolled through the gates at Bracebridge Street.

Norton, like the rest of the world, had spent the better part of the 1960s in almost constant turmoil. Norton was consolidated with AMC (Associated Motorcycles Group) in 1962. In 1966, the industrial giant Manganese Bronze Holdings Limited purchased AMC. Five marques were included: AJS, Matchless, Francis Barnett, James and of course, Norton. The new concern was to be called Norton-Matchless Ltd. This joining of the companies began a period of mixing and matching components. Basically, one motor and/or frame was used for several models. The 750 Norton Atlas begat the AJS model 33 and the Matchless G15. These bikes used the same Atlas engine, the same AMC frame and Norton Roadholder forks and front brakes, and they managed to offend almost everyone; they weren't really Nortons, AJs or Matchlesses. The outcome of this marketing debacle was yet another change; Matchless, AJS and the others, none of which had even made their own bikes for almost five years, were folded, and a new company was formed: Norton-Villiers.

The Atlas was a good motorcycle, fast, sure-footed and fairly reliable. Its one glaring fault was engine vibration, which frequently caused premature fatiguing to electrical systems, brackets, body work and often, the rider. N-V strategists knew that they had to come up with something better if, facing increasing competition from Japan, they wanted to stay in the motorcycle business much longer. They explored two options. The first was the dormant P-10, a two-cylinder, 800cc double overhead cam engine that had been

started but never finished. Though it showed promise, financial and time constraints put it to rest, at least for the time being. The other tack was a thorough rehash of the venerable Atlas. Dr. Stefan Bauer, then head of engineering, chose plan B.

The project commenced in January of 1967. The first Commando was seen at the Earl's Court show in September of that year. Resplendent in silver metalflake, the Commando was the talk of the show. Bauer had three objectives in mind: little or no vibration; an irresistible look; and superior performance. The basic 750 motor already had plenty of horsepower, and most if not all of the bugs had been worked out. Nortons were already famous for their forks and brakes, so they were used more or less without changes. Styling could always be adjusted, but looks had never been a problem for Norton. The vibration

problem, however, was the sticking point. The solution was elegant in its simplicity: Let the motor shake, the good doctor reasoned; just don't let any of the vibration get through to the rider.

And so began the Isolastic System. Norton designed a frame that hung the engine, transmission, and swingarm from a series of rubber bushings. These were shimmed to provide limited lateral movement. The result was spectacular – literally no vibration reached the rider or passenger.

With the Isolastic System in place, the motor received some minor upgrades, as did the gearbox. The new bike handled well (although some diehards claim not as well as the older "featherbed"-framed machines), and had an abundance of power. As for the styling, it was superb. The first machines hit the road in 1968, styled as the 20M3 – later known as "the Fastback." Later models lost the wrap-around seat and became known as Roadsters. Other versions were the LR, or Long Range (large tank); the Street Scrambler (high pipes); the Highway (touring

version); the High Rider (a pseudo-chopper); and the racers: the 750cc production, the fully faired John Player Special and the rarely seen Thruxton Club Racer.

Right from the start the Commando series was highly desirable. It was voted Bike of the Year four times (1968-1971) in a reader's poll sponsored by England's prestigious *Motor Cycle News*. The Commando story is not all sweetness and light, however. In 1972, the Combat engine option was released, and to the company's horror, under certain circumstances these engines self-destructed within a matter of miles. As one pundit said, "These are grenades looking for a war." Norton had to eat the lot of them, but in the end the bike was better for it.

In 1973, the engine displacement was increased to 850cc and in 1975, the Commando acquired an electric start. The last models were made in 1977. From the original Bert Hopwood-designed 500cc Twin of 1948 to the last Commando of 1977, Norton's big twin had had a run of almost 30 years.

ABOVE LEFT TOP An engine detail of the first series Commando, the 20M3. The points, situated where the magneto used to be, were later moved to the end of the camshaft, where the tach drive is in this photo.

ABOVE LEFT The 1974 John Player Replica was rare at the time and is even rarer now. The fiberglass enclosure hid a steel gas tank.

ABOVE The first edition of the Commando, the 1968 Fastback. The road holder forks and the twin leading shoe front brake were lifted from the Atlas.

The Triumph Trident

The first American road test of the new Triumph Trident (T150) was reported in the October 1968 issue of *Cycle World* magazine. The reviewer called it "a big, fast ground-shaker of a motorcycle." The last line of the article was emphatic: "There isn't another motorcycle like it!" (Actually, there was. The BSA Rocket 3 was almost identical, but that's another story.)

The Trident was originally conceived by engineer Bert Hopwood in 1963. As Hopwood told it, he and his partner, Doug Hele, laid out the basic design just to amuse themselves one night after hours. When rumors of Honda's soon-to-be-released flagship 750 became too credible to ignore around 1964, the decision was made to proceed with the three-cylinder "Tiger and a Half," as it was then known.

Unfortunately, no one knew how many cylinders or what configuration the new Honda was to have, or events might have proceeded differently.

By 1965 the prototype was up and running. Only slightly wider and just forty pounds heavier than a 650 twin, the new engine made 58hp. It fit nicely into a standard 650 frame, and according to Hopwood, the bike could have gone into production in that form in time for the 1965 selling season. But management had a different idea, because the Triple was intended to carry the marque of both Triumph and its parent company, BSA. The styling was farmed out to a British design firm called Ogle, which worked primarily in the auto industry. They replaced the classic and distinctively rounded Triumph fuel tank with a square one, the "breadloaf," and removed the

PREVIOUS PAGES The
Trident's muffler was ugly,
but it worked very well
and was used in production
racing for a number of years.
The placement of the horn
behind the right passenger
peg seemed to be an after-
thought.

BELOW The Hurricane's
fiberglass body was molded
in two halves: The seam
ran down the middle, hence
the broad band in the center
of the tank.

traditional, spirited mufflers and installed a set that
looked like they were pirated from a 1953 Buick, the
infamous "ray-guns," or as the Americans came to call
them, "Flash Gordons."

The bike was released in this state in the fall
of 1968. While the styling certainly took some getting
used to, the performance was right on the mark. The
new bike would run an honest 120 mph day in and
day out and turn the quarter-mile in 13 seconds.
The brakes were found wanting — after all, they were
designed to stop a Bonneville that weighed almost
100 pounds less — and low-speed handling was ham-
pered by that same extra poundage. All in all, the bike
received good if not outstanding reviews. But sales
were rather slow. The styling put many people off, as
did the $1,750 price tag. The point of no return came
in October of 1968 (the same month as *Cycle World's*

test report), when Honda announced that its new
750 would have four cylinders, five speeds, a disc
brake, an electric starter, and would retail for almost
$250 less than the three-cylinder, four-speed, drum-
braked and kick-started Trident.

The new Triple (both BSA and Triumph versions) was beset by petty problems right from the
start, which didn't help matters. The "bits-and-pieces"
approach to building a motorcycle that typified
British engineering at the time was a large part of the
problem. The Triple's crankcases were made up in
three sections: crankcase, inner primary case and
timing cover. Add in the outer primary and the outer
timing cover and you have four vertical joints, all
of which could, and often did, leak oil. Primary align-
ment of the clutch and crank gear was crucial, and
often misaligned, resulting in a short clutch center

life. Despite a good-sized oil cooler that kept engine heat at bay, some of the early models experienced rapid valve, piston and ring wear.

For all of that, the Triples were outstanding performers both on the street and at the racetrack, trouncing the relatively poor-handling Japanese bikes with some regularity. One machine, nicknamed "Slippery Sam" (after blowing an oil line and covering the machine and rider with oil) won the Isle of Man 750 TT production race five times. Triples were also winners in the Isle of Man Formula 750 race twice. In the United States, they were more successful at the amateur and semi-pro end than they were in the pro ranks, although Dick Mann won Daytona in 1972 on a BSA-badged Triple.

In 1970, Triumph, realizing the error of its styling ways, offered its dealers a "beauty" kit. For 1970, the kit included a traditional 3.5-gallon tank, new mufflers, fenders, stays and exposed spring shocks. The kit was an instant success; it instantly transformed the ugly duckling into the swan it was meant to be. The kit, which was also offered at a low price to owners of the early machines, actually copied the best styling cues of the 1965 prototype. At the same time, the factory started to upgrade the bike's reliability as well. Better casting techniques eliminated

most of the oil leaks, better pistons and rings were used and more durable valves were installed to prolong engine life. In fact *Cycle* magazine interviewed one proud owner who had covered 100,000 miles with only routine maintenance, and the occasional top end job.

By 1972, the Trident had grown a fifth speed. A factory blockade halted most production for 1973 and few bikes made it to the showroom floor. The Tridents that were sold had a sorely needed front disc brake. The 1974 Trident was probably the best of the lot, unchanged except for the paint. It was one of the fastest bikes in the world, it stopped well, the handling was flawless and it was as reliable as anything on the road. The 1975 model was another story. Listed as the T160, it came with the inclined motor of the BSA and offered an electric starter. Neither feature was an advantage and the bikes sold poorly. By 1976, the Trident was pretty and heavy, and it was slow, the result in the United States of Environmental Protection Agency-mandated mufflers. Its fuel mileage, never good in the best of times, was downright poor. In 1977 it was dropped from the line. Highly collectible today, the original version, with breadloaf tank and ray-gun mufflers, is ironically the most sought-after model.

ABOVE The off side of the 1972 Hurricane. The front brake is the late (and unloved) conical hub version. The front forks were slightly longer than stock. The seat was held on with Velcro to allow easy access to storage space. Since the bike was based on the BSA variant of the Triple, the engine was sloped forward slightly, more for styling than function. The wheels were Akront alloys. The Hurricanes were only sold for one year,1972; all told, only 1171 were built.

The Honda CB750

BELOW The four pipes say
it all. Unusual for a Japanese
motorcycle, the 750/4 used
dry sump lubrication, with
the tank and lines much like
contemporary British bikes.

OPPOSITE A 1970 750
Honda. The 750 served
notice to the rest of the
world that the Japanese
were serious about building
motorcycles.

When Honda introduced its flagship model, the CB750, on June 6, 1969, it tipped the motorcycling world on its collective ear. It had four cylinders, each with its own carb, pipe, overhead cam (a Honda trademark), five-speed transmission, hydraulic front disc brake and to top it all off, an electric starter. All of this was wrapped up in a highly attractive package that was as pretty as it was fast. Developing 68 horsepower at 8,000 rpm and singing one of the sweetest songs this side of heaven, the new Honda was an instant success. Here at last was Honda's near-legendary reliability allied with blistering performance. High performance motorcycles, until then, had always meant high maintenance, and Honda had always felt that the two should be mutually exclusive. Quite simply, the CB750 was a "turnkey" performance motorcycle, as reliable and requiring about the same amount of tinkering as the family sedan.

The best thing about the new 750 was its amazing versatility. You could use its stunning and abundant power to go road racing, touring, drag racing or simply to run errands, and many owners did all four and then some. The big 750 spawned an entire aftermarket devoted solely to its care. Parts to build anything from a full-dress touring bike to an all-out Grand Prix racer were readily available. The bike wasn't perfect; while the 750 was fast and smooth, its handling was never on a par with the big British bikes, and the early ones also had a nasty habit of throwing their drive chains through the cases when subject to an overly exuberant throttle. But for the most part, their fans deemed them pretty close to perfect.

In the Honda tradition, the bike underwent slow but continual development. Improved throttle linkage made synchronizing the carbs easier. The ignition switch was moved from under the tank, an awkward spot, to a console on the top clamp. While these may seem like inconsequential changes (and there were dozens more), they added up to a bike that was exceedingly civilized and offered a high degree of performance. By 1972, the CB750 had been dethroned as the performance king, as other bikes emerged that were faster and handled better. The Honda was still popular, though, and sold well through the 1970s.

In 1975, Honda released the first Super Sport version of the 750. This model had a four-into-one pipe and a host of styling changes. The following year saw the last of the traditionally styled 750s. In 1979, Honda released the CB750F, a double overhead-cam, 16-valve machine that was considered to be the pinnacle of the Honda 750. Today, the bike that created the whole genre of Japanese four-cylinders lives on in the Nighthawk 750, a bike that Honda considers an "entry level" bike.

OPPOSITE In its day the 750 was considered somewhat wide. The alternator was situated under the left side cover, increasing engine width.

LEFT The bike that put Honda on the map in the United States: The CL77 Scrambler.

BELOW The lessons learned in building the 305cc Super Hawk were put to good use in the design of the 750/4. The engine was similar to that of the Scramblers – a single overhead cam in unit with a four-speed transmission. The Super Hawk often humbled bikes twice its size in impromptu races.

The Kawasaki H1 Mach III 500 and H2 Mach IV 750

RIGHT The '69 Kawasaki H1's sedate appearance belied its true no-nonsense character. The exhaust pipe routing took some getting used to: the right side had two pipes, the left, one. The clear tube on the back side of the oil tank shows how much oil is left, tough to check at speed. Compare the front brake to the one on the '65 Bonneville.

OPPOSITE As if the stock motor wasn't enough, this owner fitted expansion chambers and K&N air filters to his 1971 H1. Anticipating the bike's ferocious acceleration, he also mounted flat "drag" handlebars. The effectiveness of the steering dampener is debatable, in part because the front wheel spends as much time off the ground as on it.

The designers at Kawasaki who created the Mach III must have heard people say that motorcycles are fun because they "wheelie." Wheelie it did – and with a vengeance! In 1965, Kawasaki opened for business in the United States. Being a relative newcomer, the firm wanted to make its name known as quickly as possible. A line of high performance two-strokes seemed to be the way to go. The 250 Samurai and the 350 Avenger got them off to a good start. By 1969, they were ready to try something bigger. The Kawasaki H1 (otherwise known as the Mach III) was designed right from the start as a no-holds-barred, high performance motorcycle. The H1's three-cylinder two-stroke engine made 60hp at 8,000 rpm and was capable of 125 mph. It weighed just about 400 pounds and had a 55-inch wheelbase. The net result was a motorcycle that was extraordinarily fast, with a

heavy rear weight bias and quick steering. The end product was a bike with "twitchy" steering and a tendency to wheelie at the slightest provocation. Speed was definitely the H1's forte. Its handling was notoriously bad. Braking was for all purposes nonexistent; the front brake was a measly 7.9-inch double leading shoe (slightly smaller than the one on a 1969 Triumph 500, a bike barely capable of 100 mph). Clamp it on hard and the lever was just as likely to come straight back to the handlebar as to stop you. The H1 was built for one thing and one thing only: heart-stopping, arm-wrenching acceleration. Kawasaki claimed that the H1 would turn a 12.4 quarter-mile straight out of the box – and it was true!

Unfortunately, the H1 also had a fair appetite for self-destruction, and not just from crashing. Its crankshaft was prone to big end failure, and the top end

ABOVE The H2 750 had the same basic design as the 500 but offered even more performance. In theory, the forward cant of the engine was to help keep the front wheel on the ground during acceleration; in reality, it rarely did. The large cable exiting the engine case operates the oil pump.

RIGHT The bosses on the lower right fork tube were for an optional second caliper, a worthy addition. The framework looks a bit spindly, and it is. The H's shared one common trait: speed and acceleration came first, while braking and handling were a distant second.

had to be rebuilt on a fairly regular basis. The early bikes used a capacitive discharge ignition system (along with surface gap plugs) that were also somewhat less than reliable. In a retrograde step, these were swapped for points in the later models (although, curiously, the H2 750 model kept the CDI system). By 1972, the H1 had been toned down somewhat and had acquired a front-disc brake. While this did much to inspire rider confidence, it was only marginally better at stopping the bike. In 1972, the H1 sired two offspring, the H2 750 Mach IV and the 350 Mach II. (A third model, the S11 250 triple would come later). The H2 750 was an unprecedented exercise in excess. It weighed just slightly more (422 pounds) than the H1 and made 74 horsepower, phenomenal for that time. It would run the quarter-mile in 12 seconds flat. Not surprisingly, the handling, or rather the lack of it, was even more exaggerated.

In contrast, the 350 was a pleasant little bike, better known for its light steering and good handling than for its speed. By the mid-1970s, both the H1 and H2 had been discontinued. Tightened noise and exhaust emission standards, as well as the success of Kawasaki's four-stroke models, would lay them to rest. But in every possible way, they had put Kawasaki squarely on the map.

The Kawasaki Z1

RIGHT The Eddie Lawson
Replica, built to win the U.S.
Superbike Championship.
The 1982 1000cc ELR was
available in two versions: the
cosmetically enhanced
KZ1000R and the genuine
racer KZ1000SI.

OPPOSITE The King, the
'73 Z1 combined raw power
with decent handling. It also
started the trend towards
UJMs – Universal Japanese
Motorcycles. Outside of its
double overhead cams and
spark plug placement, it
could almost be the 750
Honda's larger and fiercer
brother.

When Honda released its 750/4 in 1972, Kawasaki strategists were devastated. Its new flagship motor was sitting in the California apartment of Sam Tanegashima, one of Kawasaki's development engineers assigned to what was then known as "The New York Steak" project. The telex from Kawasaki headquarters was terse and to the point: "Drastic review of our product inevitable." Kawasaki was the acknowledged leader in the horsepower race. Its H series offered heart-stopping, mind-numbing acceleration and little else. Management knew that to be taken seriously in the world of real motorcyclists, they had to have a four-stroke engine, and frankly their W series (copies of BSA's A10 series) just wasn't going to cut it. The H series had gotten the Kawasaki name on the marquee. The Z1 would make sure that it stayed there. Back to the drawing board they went. The original design had called for an inline double overhead cam 750 four. The first thing the design team did was increase the displacement to 900cc; the big bore plus the DOHC design virtually ensured horsepower supremacy. The 903 was everything the Honda CB750 was – just more of it. In fact, during testing the Z1 often wore a Honda tank and seat. The "King" was released to the American motorcycle press late in 1972. The 82hp, 542-pound (wet) bike drew rave reviews.

Visually, the 903 was imposing. Its wet-sump design made it sit up a bit higher in the frame than the Honda and it also eliminated potential oil line leaks. The engine itself was painted black, while the outer covers were polished. The four upswept megaphones emitted little more than a whisper at idle. Its overall appearance was as clean and purposeful as a surgeon's scalpel, and in the wrong hands, could be just as dangerous. The Z1 had so much power that it had to be experienced to be believed. It would happily sit in traffic all day without a spit or sputter,

and just as happily knock off a 12-second quarter-mile. Loaded down with a fairing, bags and other requisite touring gear, it would handily do second gear wheelies. The handling still wasn't equal to Europe's best bikes, but it was easily the best handling bike ever to come from Japan, and with so much horsepower on tap, you could easily reel in all but the fastest specials on the straights.

As with the Honda, there was soon a burgeoning aftermarket to cater to the owners' wants and needs: bronze swingarm bushings to replace the quick-wearing plastic ones installed at the factory; four-into-one exhaust systems; bigger carbs; hotter cams; and lots more. By 1977 the 903 had become the KZ1000. There were numerous spin-offs along the way: police bikes, factory race replicas such as the Eddie Lawson Replica and outright racers. (The KZ1000 won the AMA Superbike Championships in 1977 and 1978.)

The Z1 was a legend in its own time and continues to be one. In concept, today's Kawasaki superbikes are direct descendants of the original Z1, and true to the original intent, the name Kawasaki has become synonymous with fast motorcycles.

ABOVE The Z1 had high, wide handlebars, the better to get a solid grip on at high speeds. The wide bars also helped cope with the Z1's weight (542 lbs) when puttering around town.

RIGHT The Z1's surly good looks and aggressive stance won it as many friends as did its tremendous horsepower.

OPPOSITE If the valve cover left you in doubt, the points cover spelled it out: double overhead cam. The massive clutch is behind the dinner-plate-sized cover.

The Ducati 750 Super Sport

Ducati has always prided itself on building no-compromise sport bikes, as well suited to the track as to the street. By and large, its GT-style bikes have always been moderate sellers at best. Its sport bikes, though, have been considered the "ne plus ultra" of motorcycling. When the Ducati 750 Super Sport was released in 1973, it was accorded instant classic status. It was also the most desirable production racer available.

Based on Ducati's Imola-winning bike of 1972, the SS boasted impressive credentials right from the start. The engine was a 90-degree V-twin; the valve actuation was unique in that it was desmodromic, or desmo for short. In the desmo engine, the valves are both opened and closed by the camshafts. The opening cycle is accomplished as one would expect; the cam lobe pushes down on a hardened lash cap setting atop the valve. To close the valve, an additional lobe is called into service. This pushes down on an inverted rocker arm with a forked end. This fork works against another adjuster (and keeper) located on the valve stem. This system obviates the need for valve springs, and their potential for unrestrained valve movement at high rpm; in short, since the valve action is controlled in an absolute and positive manner, the valves simply cannot float. The down side of this is that adjustment is time consuming, complicated and frequent. Ducati had pioneered desmodromic valve actuation (although Mercedes Benz gets the credit for the concept). It had heretofore only been used in its GP racers and the 250/350 singles of the late 1960s through the early 1970s.

The engine breathed through a pair of 40mm Dell'Orto pumper carbs; no air filters were fitted

RIGHT An instant classic, the "round case" 750SS is shown here in its most common role today: the collector's showpiece. The clear strip on the fuel tank was for checking the fuel level.

OPPOSITE The 750SS sported open Dell'Orto carbs, the definitive shaft and bevel gear cam drive and the early round primary cover – a perfect blend of form and function.

(pumper refers to the built-in accelerator pumps). A pair of Conti megaphones were thinly disguised to look like mufflers. To quicken the steering, both rims were 18 inches. The front boasted a dual-disc brake and the rear a single-disc brake. Early bikes had Lockheed components, while later ones were equipped with Scarab. The frame was a typical Ducati masterpiece; using the engine as a stressed member, it was supremely rigid. The bike simply didn't flex. Suspension, fore and aft, was capably if stiffly handled by Marzocchi. The 750SS was and is superbly rider friendly. It makes its horsepower the old-fashioned way – huge amounts of low- and mid-range torque to get you on your way, and an incredible linear flow of horsepower that seems to go on forever. Couple that to a frame that responds to the subtlest rider input and brakes that are smooth, progressive and fade-free, and you have a bike that makes a poor rider look good, a competent rider fantastic, and a good rider feel like he's gone to heaven.

To be sure, the 750SS had a few minor flaws. The switches and lights were more appropriate for a moped than for a serious bike. (The headlight was generally replaced with a number plate though, so it really didn't matter). The paint on the tank seldom matched the paint on either of the fenders (which often didn't match each other) or the fairing. The fiberglass had a disturbing tendency to stress-crack; and on the first test bike offered to *Cycle* magazine, there was actually a fly embedded in the top of the tank!

Honestly, though, no one really cared about the little details. Those big "Ducs" were meant to be ridden hard, and at that they excelled.

The BMW R90S

BMW was always considered a manufacturer of well-made, smooth, and ultra-reliable touring bikes. However, few if any of its models were of real interest to the sporting rider. Earlier efforts like the R50S and R69S represented a step in the right direction, but hadn't gone far enough. While the motors were willing (particularly in the case of the R69S), the frames were heavy, the front forks (Earl's pattern) abominable, and the brakes barely adequate. It's true that you could cruise at speeds that would leave other sportier machines and their pilots gasping for air, and that real BMW "bahnstormers" could adapt their riding styles to maneuver their flat twins quite rapidly, but riding one quickly was never the attractive proposition that, say, a quick dash on your Tiger 100 or even an A-10 could be. For the "civilized" rider, though, they were just the thing. Low maintenance, a strong, silent motor, shaft drive and a sober and

RIGHT The BMW that broke the mold: The 1974 R90S, finished in grey /smoke. The tank shape was reminiscent of the earlier models, but the performance wasn't. The kick starter was gone by 1976.

OPPOSITE In general the BMW is a lot narrower than it looks. Overall width was less than most of the Japanese fours. The stylish cockpit fairing, while offering good upper body protection, unfortunately contributed to front end instability.

impeccable finish of black or Dover white were all major selling points and made the bikes worth their high asking price.

The introduction of the /5 series in 1969 marked a new beginning for BMW. The new bikes, most notably the R75, marked a radical departure. Bright colors, a splash of chrome, light frames and resolute engines all added up to a quick, good handling machine that retained the reliability and quality of the previous models. The new range of electric-start twins were immediately popular, and like so many good handling, fast motorcycles before them, they soon found their way to the racetrack.

At the track it was found that a slight weave set in at about 90 mph, something fast street riders often complained about. The fix was simple, stiffer front springs, and by 1973, a longer swingarm. Braking left something to be desired and by 1974, power, at least on the dyno chart, was trailing the best Asian and European efforts. BMW, in a bold move that would have been unthinkable ten years earlier, introduced the R90S. For a company that had always placed a high value on restraint, the introduction of the 90S was anything but restrained. The R90S was an instant success. The specs might seem commonplace now, but in 1974, they were state of the art. The 900cc engine fed its 9.5-to-1 pistons through 38mm Dell'Orto pumper carbs and it used a new five-speed transmission to propel its 500 pounds (wet) through the quarter-mile in a mere 13 seconds. In top gear, it would easily pull away from a Kawasaki Z1, and it would do it quietly and comfortably; it would even do it with panniers on. If the pace got too hot, there were a pair of ten-inch disc brakes up front and a seven-inch drum in the rear to cool it off. Completely out of character for BMW, a handsome cockpit fairing was mounted to the front fork, which for the first time was gaiterless. The fairing held a voltmeter and

RIGHT The R100RS, introduced in 1976, was a 1000cc sport tourer. The full fairing not only offered superb weather protection, but enhanced overall stability as well. Initially the bikes were sold with spoked wheels; later models came with mags.

BELOW A Rob North-framed 1000cc racer originally built for U.S. Superbike competition by Butler and Smith, the American distributor of BMWs until 1980.

clock. The tach and speedometer were mounted in an attractive binnacle that also held a full array of warning lights. The seat was nicely tapered to complete the look. The paint scheme was gorgeous, a grey-smoke (later models were orange-smoke) which was as perfectly applied as it was unique.

Yet the R90S was not without its faults. When pushed hard on a tight, twisting road, the long travel and relatively soft springing of its suspension sometimes caused the bike to lose its composure. However, it compensated by behaving extremely well under most conditions and giving a supremely comfortable ride to boot. It also had a tendency to use some oil,

but this was eventually rectified by modifying the crankcase breather.

The R90S did well in production class racing. Machines prepared by the American importer Butler and Smith finished first and second in the 1976 Daytona Superbike race, and won the American Superbike championship that same year. The influence of the R90S can still be seen in the new generation of boxer motor BMW sport bikes. Had the 90S been a failure, it's doubtful that the factory would have tried something so out of character again. That it didn't, and they did, demonstrates just how right the original concept was.

ABOVE The engine bay of a 1978 R100RS. The traditional round valve covers were replaced by the square style in 1976. All of the 1000cc bikes used Bing constant velocity carburetors. The full fairing complicated servicing, but offered outstanding protection from the elements.

The Moto Guzzi 850 LeMans

Released in 1976, the Moto Guzzi 850 LeMans was an instant success. A capable performer on both the street and the track, the LeMans soon attracted a loyal following. The engine was a revamped version of Moto Guzzi's original 700cc V-twin. Punched out to 850cc, the new engine was tractable, easy to maintain, and made enough horsepower to cruise in the triple digits any time the rider felt the urge. The frame was a simple double-cradle affair, flex-free, narrow and easy to produce. Because the final drive was by drive shaft (which causes the rear of the motorcycle to rise and fall as power is applied and reduced), the suspension was set up on the firm side. This practically eliminated the pitch and resultant loss of stability that plagues many shaft-driven bikes when ridden hard. The three disc brakes operated in a unique way. The foot pedal operated the rear brake and left front; when the need arose, the handlebar lever operated an additional right side front brake. It took some getting used to, but worked well. The body work was pure "cafe racer" – clip-on bars, a bikini fairing, mag wheels and a bright red paint job. *Cycle* magazine called it "The Flash Bike for the Thinking Man," and it was: stunning performance, lovely to look at, and eminently practical (for a superbike).

The Guzzis' secret was the use of the reliable V-twin 850 motor to power a new chassis. By now it is well known that the original V-7 motor was originally designed to power a small Jeep-like "mechanical mule" for NATO. Guzzi's chief of design, Giulio Caracano, realized that the ideal design was going to be air-cooled, compact, have a high power-to-weight ratio, possess the reliability of an anvil and be easy to repair if it did break. When the NATO deal fell through, Caracano made the V-7 the basis of his motorcycle engine.

Caracano's main interest was Grand Prix racing, but he knew that the bills must be paid, no matter

what. He also knew that big, reliable motorcycles were popular with armies, police forces and Americans, all of whom paid their bills. Enter the V-7. Solid and trucklike probably describe these touring versions best. In the early 1970s it was decided to build a production racer. Caracano retired shortly before the 1972 introduction of the V-7 Sport. His successor was Lino Tonti, a talented racer and engineer who had actually done most of the detail work on the Sport, including the new frame. Tonti had actually crashed one prototype, breaking his leg in the process, and supposedly finished the design from his hospital bed. The logical outcome of the V-7 was the LeMans, introduced in 1976. The engine was a warmed-up version of the basic T-3 touring bikes. The frame was a masterpiece of rigidity. The linked brakes worked surprisingly well; the foot pedal, which typically activated only the rear brake, did extra duty on this bike

RIGHT As lean as a two-by-four, the 1976 LeMans was only slightly more comfortable. The LeMans was just the thing for fast road work. The swan neck clip-ons offered a degree of comfort not found on most cafe racers. For those long-legged individuals who may have found the valve covers intrusive, Moto Guzzi offered bolt-on knee pads.

OPPOSITE The GP influence is obvious in the tank styling. Dell'Orto pumper carbs are run without filters, not exactly conducive to long engine life – most owners fit some style of aftermarket filter.

and controlled one of the two front brake discs, as well. When the pedal was depressed, 30 percent of the front brake and 70 percent the rear brake were activated. Meanwhile, the handlebar lever controlled the second front disc. Despite the road-race-style crouch, the LeMans made a pretty good touring bike. Its engine was just as happy to plod along the highway as it was to charge through the canyon at full speed. That the bike was one of the best handlers in the world should have been expected, particularly in light of Tonti's past experiences. That it did it with shaft final drive was astounding. In fact, the shaft was unnoticeable as far as handling went, neither rising nor falling as the throttle was used.

Most of the owners' complaints centered on detail items: the switch gear and paint were disappointing, and the nicely styled seat would split almost immediately. On the plus side, the 850 was incredibly easy to maintain, was a glutton for punishment, offered incredibly good handling, and was fast. Able to leave the crowd behind with a twist of the throttle, it had no trouble drawing one at rest. Much sought after in its prime, the 850 LeMans is a highly regarded classic today.

LEFT Everything about the Guzzi seems massive, but in fact its light weight (513 lbs) was one of its strong points. Liberal use of alloy helped keep the bike light, although the starter (located between the shift lever and float bowl) looks hefty enough for a Mack truck. Clear float bowls were a popular accessory.

BELOW What better way to spend your Sunday than charging around on a Guzzi?

53

The Kawasaki GPz Series

In 1981, Kawasaki decided to release two full-tilt sport bikes, the GPz550 and the GPz1100. The GPz750 would follow in 1982. The GPz550 was the first of the new generation sport bikes to debut. It was bright red, with the obligatory bikini fairing, low bars and rear-set footpegs, and its double overhead cam engine was a little jewel, pumping out ten more horsepower than the standard KZ550 (which was no slouch either). Dual front discs and a single rear disc promptly brought the diminutive speedster to a halt when the pace got too hot. The front fork was air adjustable, while the rear shocks were adjustable for both preload (spring height) and dampening. All

in all, it was a pretty package that really looked the part. And it ran as well as it looked. A strong motor, positive handling and progressive and fade-free brakes all added up to an instant winner; the GPz quickly became the bike to beat in 550 class production racing. On the street, many a large-bore rider was humiliated when he found that the bike he'd been struggling to keep up with through the "twisties" was "only" a 550.

On the down side, the GPz550 was a wee bit short on ground clearance, mainly because it handled so well. An accomplished rider with more brio than brains would soon find himself dragging both stands,

RIGHT Lean and mean, the Uni-Track '83 GPz750. The GPz had a host of racetrack touches: the box section aluminum swingarm with eccentric chain adjusters were straight off the racetrack.

OPPOSITE The typical GPz, a little scruffy perhaps, but still ready to take all comers. The Kerker 4-1 exhaust and K&N air filters were often the first owner-made mods.

the brake pedal, the footpegs, the exhaust flanges and eventually, as the 550 slid along on its pipes with both wheels an inch above the ground, his head. In 1982, the GPz550 would become the first Kawasaki street bike to get a single-shock rear suspension. It would continue in this form until 1984, when the production run ended.

The GPz1100 was released at the same time. It was similar in appearance, although without the fairing. The GPz1100 was created to challenge the Suzuki GS1100's claim to the title of the world's fastest street bike. In the game of technological one-upmanship, fuel injection is always better than a carburetor. Accordingly, Kawasaki endowed the 1100 with a system that it had first used on the Z-1 classic of 1981. Fuel injection works fine; unhappily, the bugs weren't quite worked out of Kawasaki's system and the bikes had a slight hesitation just off idle. The largest GPz also had some odd low-speed handling characteristics (later traced to the factory's choice of tires). The GPz1100 came very close to the GS1100, but in the end, the Suzuki stayed a lick ahead – about .4 of a second in the quarter-mile, and with a definite edge in the handling department. Kawasaki would keep adding fuel to the fire, however, and eventually come out on top.

The third member of the GPz triumvirate was the GPz750. The 750 class had been considered moribund for several years. Attention had been focused largely on the 1000cc-and-up class, and for good reason: big bikes, big performance and for the manufacturers, big money. For a variety of reasons (a return to the 750cc limit for superbike racing in the United States, for one), interest in the 3/4-liter bikes gained ground in the early 1980s. Kawasaki, having had great success with its GPz550 (and only moderate success with its 1100), decided the time was right for something in between. The obvious choice? A 750. In designing the GPz750, Kawasaki used exactly what had worked so well in the past: a stout, albeit light frame, responsive steering geometry, strong brakes, and a powerful engine. A flashy coat of red paint and good ergonomics rounded out the picture.

The GPz750 reached a new plateau; easily the fastest and best handling 750 of its day, the GPz would eventually spin off into the ZXR750s. The GPz series was really the last of the "touring" superbikes. As sport bikes progressed, they tended to become more narrowly focused; the GPzs were a transitional bike in that they made passable touring bikes. As the performance wars heated up, that, too, would change.

The Honda V45 Interceptor

Early superbikes were as much a product of evolution as of revolution. The production model begat the race bike, which led to an improved version of the street bike, which turned back into another version of the race bike, ad infinitum. In 1983, the displacement limit for Superbike racing in the United States was going to be 750cc. The rules also required stock frames and standard wheel sizes.

Honda, well aware of the old axiom "win on Sunday, sell on Monday," decided to get serious about winning the U.S. championship. To do so would require a new motorcycle. The air-cooled CB750F could have been pressed into service, and many privateers did just that, but they also finished well back in the pack. Honda had debuted the first V45 Sabre in 1982, a compromise sport-touring bike. The water-cooled, shaft-driven Sabre had proven only one thing: Honda's latest engine, the V-4, worked just fine. The V-4 laid the groundwork for Honda's new racer. The V45 Interceptor was released in 1983, just in time for Daytona. The Interceptor finished 1-2-3 in the Superbike race. Honda's Interceptor had been designed from the ground up as a race bike platform. In concept as well as practice, the privateer could buy a bike off the showroom floor, and with a few minor modifications, win races. In reality, this was

RIGHT The 1983 Interceptor was the first street bike to utilize a perimeter frame. The lower radiator is located beneath the bottom fairing. While it looks cramped, the V45 was fairly easy to work on.

OPPOSITE The V might just as well have stood for victory. The V45 was a champion right from the start. Honda announced the Interceptor in full-page ads that promised to "Bring the World to Your Knees," a reference to the new bike's unparalleled handling ability. They also promised to bring the competition to their knees. At Daytona that year (1983) the Interceptor finished first, second and third in the Superbike race.

tempered by the depth of the owner's wallet, as well as the depth of his talents.

While the V45 (or VF750F as it was known officially) was neither the smallest nor lightest bike in its class, it was certainly the "trickest." A perimeter frame made of square tubing was the starting point, patterned after Honda's Formula 1 efforts. It was rigid, light and designed to enhance serviceability, either trackside or at the dealership. While the basic engine design was lifted from the Sabre, the VF used redesigned crankcases, in part to allow the engine to be rotated up and back so a shorter wheelbase could be used, and in part because the Interceptor used chain final drive. The Interceptor used the same engine internals as the Sabre: cam timing, a less restrictive exhaust and a larger air box accounted for an increase of 12 hp over the Sabre (77 vs. 65). A 16-inch front wheel provided quick yet stable steering; the rear wheel was a more prosaic 18 inches. Dual front discs and a single rear disc provided abundant stopping power; all three calipers were twin piston.

The left fork held a four-way adjustable anti-dive system, while the right fork contained the adjustable dampener. Both of the massive 39mm fork tubes were interconnected to simplify air-adjustability. The rear used a rising rate system, Pro-Link, and featured a massive cast aluminum swingarm. A unique anti-lock clutch was used; snapping a quick down-shift would allow the clutch to slip slightly, preventing rear-wheel chatter. Twin radiators were used, one mounted above the front head and one just in front of the crankcase.

The VFR750 was an instant success both on the track and in the showroom, much more so than its immediate predecessor, the FWS (a 1000cc Formula 1 version used as a test bed). The VF would grow both up and down over the next few years; the tariff-beating 700s, the VF30 500cc version (probably the most user-friendly bike of the lot) and the VF1000 all left their mark on the sport bike scene. Currently the Interceptor is available as the VFR750, considered one of the best sports motorcycles in the world.

OPPOSITE The left side frame rail unbolted to facilitate engine removal. Safety wire would indicate that this particular bike has seen some combat experience.

BELOW By current standards, the Interceptor looks rather naked. The tail section was an option. The 16-inch front wheel was radical for its time.

The Ducati 750 F1 Series

The Ducati F1A and F1B were true race replicas, street-going versions of the first of the "rubber band racers," the four-time world champion 600cc TT2. The TT2 was built for the 1981 Formula 2 World Championship. With British racer Tony Rutter on board, they won not only the 1981 championship, but the 1982, 1983 and 1984 championships as well. In 1982, Fabio Taglioni, chief of design, and Franco Farne, race team boss, decided to develop concurrently a 750cc racer to compete in Formula 1. While the 750 was never as competitive in Formula 1 as its smaller stablemate had been in Formula 2, it soon proved to be the hot set for the newly formed and very popular "Battle of the Twins" class. The bikes did exceptionally well in both club races and world championship events.

Before long, enthusiasts began to clamor for a road-going version of the race bikes, preferably the 750. At the same time, Ducati street bikes had lost their edge; they were no longer the sharply focused sport bikes they had once been. In fact, they were shadows of their former selves and losing more ground on the sales floor to the Japanese every day. In 1985, Ducati decided to build the machine that would ultimately put it back on top – the racer-replica F1A. Unfortunately, 1985 saw Ducati caught between a rock and a hard place. The company was having financial trouble; poor management had taken its toll. It was still in business, making engines for the fast-growing Cagiva concern. But outside of its race bikes and the new F1, it really had nothing left. The F1 was seen by many as a final act of defiance, a dying gladiator's wave to the crowd, a last message to the motorcycle world: "Look what you'll be

RIGHT A nicely restored 1986 F1B. Like the mythical phoenix, the F1's rose from the ashes to resurrect a dying Ducati. The birdcage frame was new, as were the belt-driven cams.

OPPOSITE The F1's used top-shelf hardware. The wheels are Marvic. Brakes are by Brembo, with floating rotors. The front fork is Marzocchi, as is the rear shock. The clutch is hydraulic, easing some of the strain on the rider. Not the most comfortable bike in the world perhaps, but it was certainly one of the best performing.

missing when we're gone."

Fortune, however, smiled on the company, and early in 1985 Cagiva purchased what was left of Ducati. (It would actually take over in May of that year, but that's another story.) In the interim, Marco Lucchinelli rode an F1A to second place at Daytona's Battle of the Twins, beaten only by the sheer horse-power of Gene Church's 1000cc Harley-Davidson, the famed "Lucifer's Hammer." (In 1986, on an 850 version, he would win it outright.) The American "Battle of the Twins" series soon became a Ducati benefit. Racetrack successes sold bikes. Wins at Laguna Seca (California), the Barcelona 24-Hour and the opening round of Formula 1 (in Italy) all helped renew interest in the marque.

In 1986, the F1B was released, which was essen-tially the same as the A model. For those who wanted something a bit more exotic – and 25 percent more expensive – Ducati offered a series of hand-built limit-ed-production versions of the F series. These bikes – the Montjuich (1986), the Laguna Seca (1987) and the Santa Monica (1988) – had about 10 mph over a standard F (137 mph vs. 127 mph) and were intended solely for the track (although many were set up for the street). In 1987, the 750 Paso was released. Based on the F1's engine, the Paso was a bit more mainstream than the racer-replica F1 series. It was also a great seller, especially by Ducati standards. As the profits flowed in, new and innovative designs were produced, culminating in outstanding motorcy-cles such as the 851 Sport (1991), the 900 Superlight (1993) and the 916. The F series, intended as a "going-away present," revitalized an on-the-ropes Ducati, and that may well be its greatest contribution to motorcycling.

The Suzuki GSX-R750 and GSX-R1100

n 1985 Suzuki decided to make a point: although its current line-up was a bit long in the tooth, the company was entirely capable of building bikes that pushed the performance envelope.

The GSX-R made its first appearance in 750 guise. Because the bike was released first in Europe, American sport-bike riders could only lick their chops and wait. When the first GSX-Rs arrived in the United States late in the fall of 1985, enthusiasts agreed that the wait had been well worth it. The GSX-R series was as single purpose as any European sport bike had ever been and twice as fast. To understand how really fast these bikes were, consider this: in the United States either version of the GSX-R could easily exceed the national speed limit of 55 mph in first gear while standing nearly vertical on its rear wheel. The secret to its success, however, was not overwhelming horsepower; in fact, at 89.5 bhp, the

1100 had less horsepower than any of its competitors and it had 11 bhp less than the bike it replaced, the GS1150. The 750's bhp rating was likewise lower than that of other bikes in its class. Why then were they such good motorcycles, able to out-accelerate, out-brake, and out-handle 99 percent of the other bikes in the world? Because they were lighter.

The GSXs were simply the lightest bikes, not only in their respective classes but in displacement classes below them as well. The 1100, for instance, was 107 pounds lighter than Honda's VR1000R, and 21 pounds lighter than the aluminum-framed Interceptor 503 to 505 (both with full fuel tanks). The 750 weighed in at a svelte 465.5 pounds, again with a full tank. The specs for both of the Rs were almost identical. The full-perimeter aluminum frame, rake, trail and wheelbase were for the most part identical. The front fork tubes were a massive 41mm. The 1100 was equipped with an electronic anti-dive; the 750 wasn't (the antidive was built-in). Both forks were adjustable for preload. The swingarm was also aluminum and its single shock was adjustable for both rebound and dampening.

The rims were 18 inches front and rear. The 1100's were the widest ever offered on a production motorcycle, 2.75 x 18 front, 4.00 x 18 at the rear. The 750's were a more common 2.50 and 3.50 respectively. Both bikes wore dual discs, with four-piston calipers up front, and a single disc in the back. The 1100s had a conventional single-piston rear caliper, while the 750, perhaps with an eye toward its career as a race bike, got a four-piston caliper. Everything was designed to be as light as practically possible. The instrument panel, for example, was simply a sheet of alloy backed up with foam.

The real weight savings were in the engine. Suzuki decided to forgo the complexity and weight that came with water cooling. By using oil to both

BELOW The 1986 GSX-R750R, a limited edition version of the 750. The R was sold more or less ready to race and came with an air-cooled dry clutch and solo seat. The pipe is by Yoshimura.

OPPOSITE A typical owner-modified GSX-R1100. Possessed of incredible performance in stock trim, there are few GSXs that are left that way.

lubricate and cool the engine, they could eliminate all of the headaches normally associated with water cooling: namely, weight, complexity, and the biggest problem of all, the fact that water has to flow through and around the hottest portion of the engine, while oil can be sprayed directly on the interior hot spots. Suzuki used a system of jets to spray cooling oil directly on the undersides of the pistons, the valve springs and stems and the tops of the combustion chambers (externally, between the valve cover and the head). The oil was then routed through a large oil cooler, and small fins cast into the cylinder and head (which were coated with a heat-dissipating paint) removed any residual heat. The engines used four valves per cylinder and flat-side carburetors (31mm for the 750 and 34mm for the 1100). They both used a four-into-one exhaust that was as constricting as it

was quiet and usually the first item to be replaced. Transmissions were a five-speed for the 1100, and a six-speed for the 750. In 1986, a race replica version of the 750 was available with an air-cooled clutch and a few detail modifications. The 750 limit in the United States precluded racing the 1100; the 750, though, was a favorite among both club racers and privateers.

A semi-official factory version was raced in the United States under the Yoshimura banner. The high point most likely was Kevin Schwantz's victory in the 1988 Daytona 200. He completely dominated the race, lapping every other rider. If the GSX-Rs had a weak point, it was their racetrack ergonomics; a ride at legal speeds that lasted over 20 minutes was agony for riders used to a less stringent seating position. Once you turned up the wick, though, it was worth it.

PREVIOUS PAGES This '92 1100 features a full house Yoshimura motor. Extensive suspension upgrades include Performance Machine wheels and six-piston calipers, and a Yoshimura air duct kit.

OPPOSITE This '86 1100 features slightly modified bodywork.

BELOW The no-frills cockpit of the 1100. With weight at a premium, the instruments are mounted in foam and inserted into a flatstock holder.

The Yamaha FZR 1000

Initially released in 1987, the FZR quickly acquired a reputation as a serious piece of hardware. Technology that was only weeks removed from the racetrack was available to anyone who could come up with the asking price, a hefty $5,800. The first generation FZR 1000 had a few shortcomings. Handling, at least on the racetrack, left something to be desired, and the engine, while having impressive numbers, was prejudiced toward the top of the power curve. Yamaha's engineers knew what improvements should be made

to rectify the situation, and the company decided that the 1989 model would start with a total revamping of the existing motorcycle, a rare opportunity indeed.

The 1989 model underwent an extensive redesign. The wheelbase was shortened by 20mm, the frame and swingarm were redesigned, increasing overall frame integrity, the fork tube diameters were increased from 41mm to 43mm and the engine was tipped back slightly. In addition, the diameter of

RIGHT Red, white and blue with a 122hp. What more could any red-blooded sport rider want? Yamaha sent the other factories back to the drawing board when they released the 1987 FZR 1000.

OPPOSITE Looking bad in black. Capable of 10.66 in the quarter-mile and with a top speed of 165 mph, the 1994 FZR 1000 has the punch to back up its good looks. Conservative steering geometry and a longish wheelbase (58.1 inches) endow it with excellent high-speed manners. Exceptional performance and handling make the FZR a formidable opponent on the street or track.

the swingarm pivot and both axles were substantially increased. The overall effect was better handling, quicker steering, and a more stable motorcycle.

The engine got new crankcases to allow it to be rotated in the frame, and several updates to enhance overall reliability. Compression was also raised to a sky-high 12.0-1. But the big news in the engine department was spelled EXUP – Exhaust Ultimate Power Valve. The Exup system varies exhaust flow. A microprocessor operating a servomotor controls the position of a rotary valve located in the exhaust collector. At low throttle openings the valve restricts flow, increasing mid-range power. At its best, the new motor churned out 25 percent more horsepower than its predecessor. The combination of a brilliant engine and stellar chassis made the FZR 1000 the top super-bike of 1990. Yamaha has never been one to rest on

its laurels, though. The FZR has undergone continuous development. In 1990, the FZR received a few minor frame updates and a male slider front fork. In 1994, six-piston calipers were added, and with a top speed of 165 miles per hour, it needs them.

Complaints have been leveled at its uncompromising, racetrack-oriented ergonomics, but few if any prospective purchasers are concerned with the FZR's touring capabilities. In its class, it is also considered a bit slow steering, while the 26.7-degree steering head angle may be considered conservative by today's standards (24 to 25 degrees is the norm for a sport bike). It definitely helps keep the FZR stable at light speed.

The FZR may have its detractors; after all, what aspiring champion doesn't? In terms of real-world performance though, it has few challengers.

The Kawasaki ZX-11

Kawasaki has always had a reputation as a builder of fast street bikes. In fact, it has often prided itself on building the fastest bike available. But as the horsepower wars heated up, Kawasaki often found itself playing catch-up. If it built a bike with 100 hp, another company would build one with 102. In 1990, Kawasaki decided to prove once and for all who builds the fastest bikes in the world. In the spring of that year, Kawasaki released the ZX-11, the first production motorcycle to run the quarter-mile in 10.52 seconds and record a top speed of 175 mph.

The ZX-11 Ninja was without a doubt the fastest, most powerful street-legal production motor-cycle that had ever been built, and it was available at the nearest dealership. The mechanical specifications are normal enough; the 1100cc 16-valve, double overhead cam engine is as close to being aerodynamically perfect as possible. The seat is positioned on the low side. This allows the rider to crouch behind the fairing instead of looking over it. The result is an aerodynamically efficient design that increases high speed stability as well as top speed. The front brakes are a simple dual disc with four-piston calipers; the rear, a single disc, with a twin-piston caliper. The exhaust is slightly unusual, a four-into-one-into-two system. The inlet tract is another unusual part; a sealed "ram air" system

RIGHT Kawasaki has long prided itself on building the fastest motorcycles money can buy. The ZX-11 has a theoretical top speed of 188 mph.

OPPOSITE The ZX-11 is the ultimate street predator with its shark-like snout, the "Jaws" of the two-wheeled world. The duct below the headlight is the snorkel for the ram air system.

BELOW Color me gone: the only view most of us will see of a ZX-11 on the move. Every aspect of the ZX is designed to enhance performance. The turn signals are faired in to reduce drag. Nothing sticks out from behind the fairing. Even the fork legs are shrouded.

RIGHT The King of superbikes. While the title may be debatable, the facts speak for themselves. The ZX-11 is the fastest production motorcycle available. The build quality is comparable to the best in the world, and the bike's all-around versatility is undeniable. The ZX-11 is a comfortable touring bike, a mild-mannered errand runner and a full ballistic berserker all rolled into one.

pressurizes it. A rack of 40mm constant-vacuum Keihen carbs do the mixing. The engine is a simple basic design, based on long-established precepts. It also develops a stupendous 126.6 horsepower. Parked, the ZX has a definite predatory look. Its nose-down attitude is reminiscent of a fighter preparing for take-off; twist that right-side grip in low gear and the "G" forces are just about the same.

Rolling along at the legal limit, the ZX-11 is well mannered; the comfort level approaches that of the average touring bike. The exhaust is quiet; the paint job is fairly low key. There's really nothing about the bike that would arouse the local constabulary's ire in any way. Of course, the rear tire, a huge seven inches across, or maybe the speedometer, calibrated to 200 mph, might raise an eyebrow. To all appearances, it's just another motorcycle out and about – until the throttle gets a big twist.

The ZX at the top of first gear is going approximately 70 miles per hour; at the top of second, 97; third, 122. As you shift into fourth gear, you pass 146 and into fifth, as you accelerate (that's right, accelerate), the speedo hits 168. If you still have the stomach for it, you notch sixth gear; sixth is good for 176 miles per hour. If you could pull redline in sixth gear you would, at least in theory, be capable of 188 miles per hour.

If the ZX could be said to have any inherent problems, it would simply be this: the motorcycle makes so much power, is so fast, and so effortlessly makes a shambles of any speed limit, that it is almost impossible to keep yourself under control.

INDEX